I0110601

Beginner Series:

Bass Method

LEVEL I

Kaitie Sly

Violet Anamnesis Publications

San Diego, California

Violet Anamnesis Publications
15658 Bernardo Terrace Suite B
San Diego, California /92128

Beginner Series: Bass Method Level I / Kaitie Sly —1st Ed.
ISBN 978-1-944213-04-6

Table of Contents

CHAPTER

The "Bass-ics" of Electric Bass

Before we even pick up the bass, let's begin with an overview of the instrument, some of its accessories, some tips on posture, and positioning. We will go over the parts of the bass, some practical options for tuners, metronomes and strings, followed by some suggestions for posture, arm and strap positioning. This will give us a solid base to begin playing... the bass!

The Electric Bass

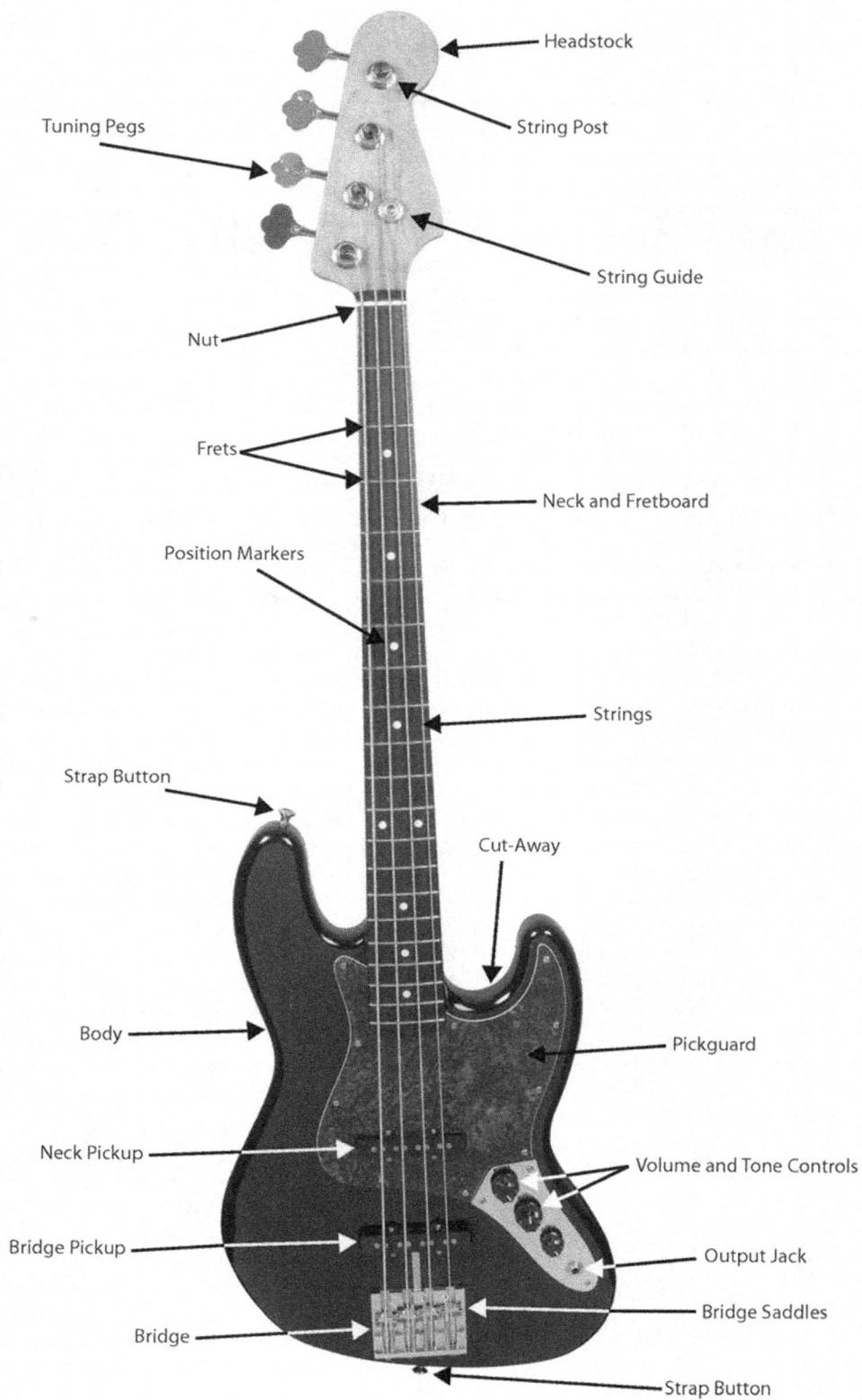

Tuning

Electric Tuners

Electric tuners are the easiest way to tune your bass.

1. Plug your bass into your tuner using an instrument cable.

2. Play your open strings one at a time – make sure the volume on your bass is turned up or the tuner won't get the signal!

3. Use the meter on your tuner to determine whether the string is sharp or flat

    o If flat (on the left hand side of the meter): tighten the string using the tuning pegs located on the head of your bass until the tuner meter is as close to centered as possible.
    o If sharp (on right hand side of center of meter): loosen the string using the tuning pegs located on the head of your bass until the tuner meter is as close to centered as possible.

Buy a cheap tuner to start - You should be able to get an electric tuner for $12-15. Make sure you get either a chromatic tuner or one for bass. Don't get the one for guitar!

iPhone or Android Apps for Tuning

These days, a lot of us have access to a smart phone or tablet. There are several different tuning "apps" that you can download onto your smart phone or tablet for tuning your instrument. Many are free and some cost a nominal fee. Some can be further enhanced by purchasing an adaptor cable to allow direct line-in access, which can dramatically improve the accuracy of the tuner.

Others work simply by listening to your instrument using the built in microphone of your device. These ones can be tricky to use sometimes because you have to be in an area that is fairly silent so that the tuner does not get confused by any ambient sounds.

I personally have been using the TC Electronic PolyTune iPhone App (www.tcelectronic.com/polytune-iphone-app/), but there are a plethora of different tuners available in the app store. Chose the one that works best for you! You can also purchase metronomes for your smart phone or tablet!

Tune to a Piano

Tuning to a piano is less precise than using a proper tuner.
  o Use the G, D, A, and E keys on the piano to check the tuning of your bass

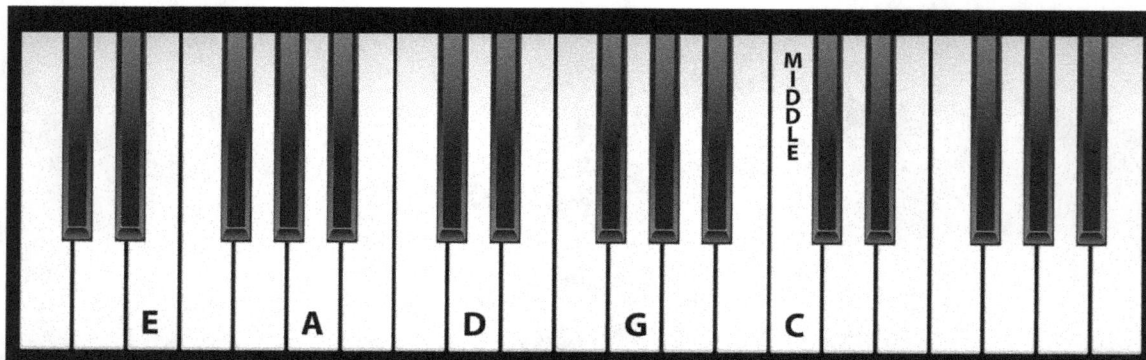

© Oculo | Dreamstime.com - Piano Keys Photo

Relative Tuning

Relative tuning is another tuning method where the strings of the bass are tuned relative to one another. It is also not as precise as using a tuner and furthermore, it assumes that the starting pitch is in tune. It will only work properly if the starting pitch is already in tune. Here we will be using the bottom E string as our starting pitch.

1. Play the 5th fret on the E string to produce the note A

2. Play the open A string to see if it sounds the same as the fretted A you just played

   o If not, tune it down or up until they sound the same
   o The closer the pitch gets, you will hear an oscillating/beating sound created by the pitches of the two notes rubbing against each other
   o The oscillating sound will stop once the notes are in pitch

3. Repeat this process for the D and G strings

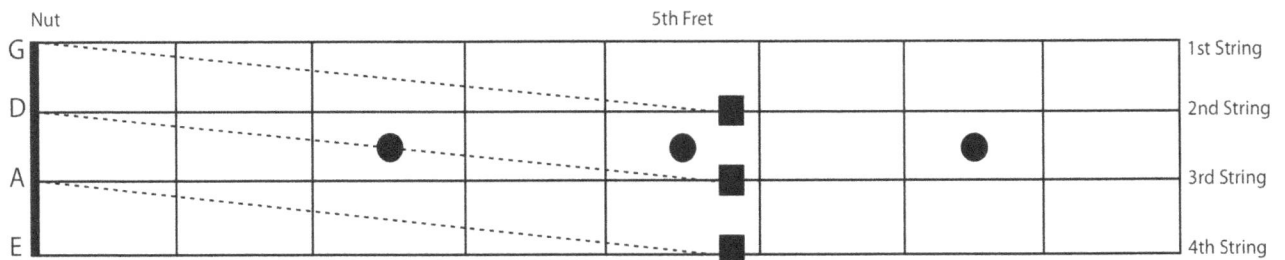

Metronomes

Since bass players are considered part of the "rhythm section," it is crucial to have a good sense of time. Bass players and drummers have to work together in a band to ensure that the songs tempo doesn't turn into a train wreck! Therefore, the metronome should be your best friend!

As mentioned above, you can download metronome apps for your smart phone or tablet so that you can have good timing wherever you go! But there are also a variety of electronic, battery powered and analog metronomes that you can purchase as well.

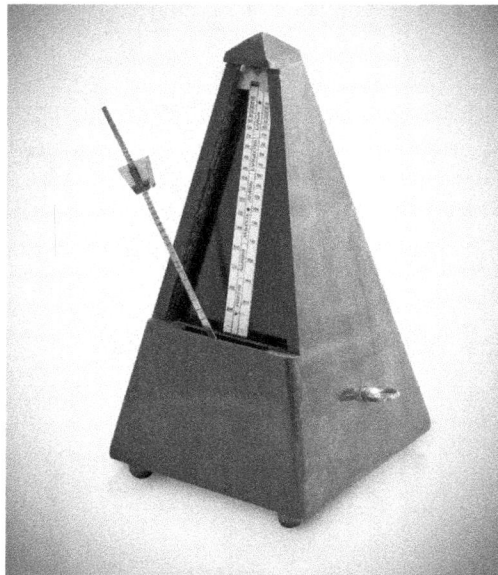

Caption: A Standard Analog Metronome

It is a good idea to learn a tune or exercise very slowly and be able to play through it correctly. After you can do this, add the metronome by setting it to a slow tempo (i.e. 50 beats per minute) and use the metronome click as the quarter note pulse.

1. Practice reading the music along with the click without your bass first.
2. Once you get the hang of it, pick up your bass and try playing along with the metronome.
3. As you get more comfortable with the piece of music, gradually increase the tempo on the metronome.

Strings

Another item on the bass to consider is the strings. There are two kinds of strings: flatwound and roundwound.

Flatwound strings are made of a steel core wire wrapped with a flat wire that has a smooth feel. They are most often used for a jazz or old school sound, or on fretless bass because they can create the unique sliding (glissando) effect that is fretless basses are famous for. Flatwounds have a mellow, round tone.

The more common type of string used for bass playing is roundwound, which have a distinct metal sound. Roundwound strings are made either from stainless steel or nickel. Stainless steel sound the brightest and nickel have a bit softer of a tone. Because stainless steel are so bright, nickel is usually recommended because finger noises are less pronounced with nickel. Roundwound strings have a ridged texture compared to flatwound. This texture can cause some wear and tear on the bass frets over time.

Less common are the groundwound, tapewound and taperwound strings.

Changing Strings

There is no rule of thumb for when to change your strings. It entirely depends on what sort of tone you are going for, as well as how often you play your bass.

The longer the strings stay on your bass, the more dirt, grease and other particles will accumulate on the strings and the strings will begin to sound dull. Players who really like a bright tone will need to change their strings more frequently to ensure that the strings stay bright. It is also a good idea to put a fresh set of strings on your bass before a recording session.

Still, other players will find that changing the strings often may interfere with their tone. Players who love a flat, thuddy old-school tone with minimal overtones or resonance may choose not to change their strings very often. Motown bassist James Jamerson, rarely, if ever, changed his strings!

When you put a fresh pair of strings on your bass, it is a good idea to pull on them gently a few times to stretch them out a bit. New strings need to be broken in, and before this happens, you may find that new strings will go out of tune more easily because they have a tendency to keep stretching as they break in. For this reason, you may want to install new strings well in advance of any gigs to avoid tuning problems!

Choosing Strings

There are four different scale lengths to choose from: short, medium, long and extra long/super long. The length of scale depends on how long your fretboard is from the bridge saddles to the nut. If you are unsure of what your bass's scale length is, you can check manufacturer's website or measure the length between the nut and the bridge.

String Lengths:	String Scale Required:
Up to 32"	Short
32" to 34"	Medium
34" to 36"	Long
36" to 38"	Extra Long / Super Long

Most basses have a 34" long scale (i.e. Fender Precision). Examples of short scale basses (30" or 30.5") are the Hofner "violin" models or the Gibson EB bass.

String Gauges

String gauges range from ultra-light to extra heavy. The gauge is the strings diameter and it is measured in thousandths of an inch.

	G	D	A	E
Ultra / Extra Light	.030/.035	.050/.055	.070/.075	.090/.095
Light	.040	.060	.080	.100
Medium	.030	.045	.065	.085
Heavy	.050	.070	.090	.110
Extra Heavy	.055	.075	.095	.115

The heavier the gauge, the lower the tone produced. Heavy gauge strings require more strength in your fingers to play.

Strings usually come in sets, but you can also buy strings individually.

Boiling Your Strings

There is a remedy to bring dull or old bass strings back to life, which is to boil your strings to remove some of the dirt and oil from them. Boiling your strings is said to produce a much sharper, crisper and springier tone. While some people swear by this remedy, others condone it as they feel it will destroy the strings properties.

Positioning and Posture

Sitting

You can sit with your legs crossed...

or straight…

Standing

You could also play standing:

The Strap

Adjust your strap so that the bass is in roughly the same position both when sitting and standing.

- o If your strap is adjusted too low, the forearm will not be able to rest on the bass when standing, and the fingers will become too parallel to the bass.
- o If your strap is adjusted too high, strain is put on your right arm as it must cramp up when positioning your forearm over the body of your bass.

CHAPTER

2

The Right and Left Hands

Now that we've got the basics of the electric bass down, let's look at more specifically what to do with our right and left hands. We will explore the different options of plucking and picking the strings with our right hand, and what is required in each case to develop a consistent tone.

We will then look more closely at the left hand and how to properly position our fingers on the fretboard.

The Right Hand!

In the right hand:

1. Your wrist and forearm should be relaxed
2. Try to focus on using the muscles only in your fingers. Keep your arm relaxed – focus your energy on finger movement.
3. Your forearm rests on top of the body of your bass – This may be difficult or awkward with odd-shaped basses such as Flying V's or Steinbergers.

Plucking or Picking?

1. **Plucking or Fingerstyle (most common):**

   Plucking or fingerstyle produces a warm, full sound and is the most common way to play the bass with your right hand.

   Rest your thumb on either the bridge or neck pickup (whatever your preference) as this will provide an anchor for your right hand. Some players may also choose to rest their thumb on the E string or even the scratch plate.

   The thumb should be positioned mostly perpendicular to the body of the bass, pointing down.

   From here, your index and middle fingers will be used to attack the strings in an alternating fashion:

2. **Roll/drag the fleshy pad part of your fingers located approximately ¼ inch from the tip, over/across the string, following through to rest at the next string.**

   o   Resting against the next string can be used as a technique to help mute any ringing from the adjacent string

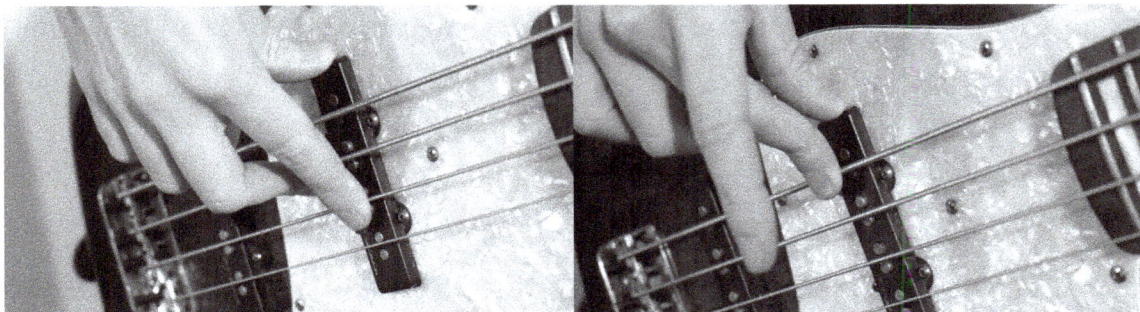

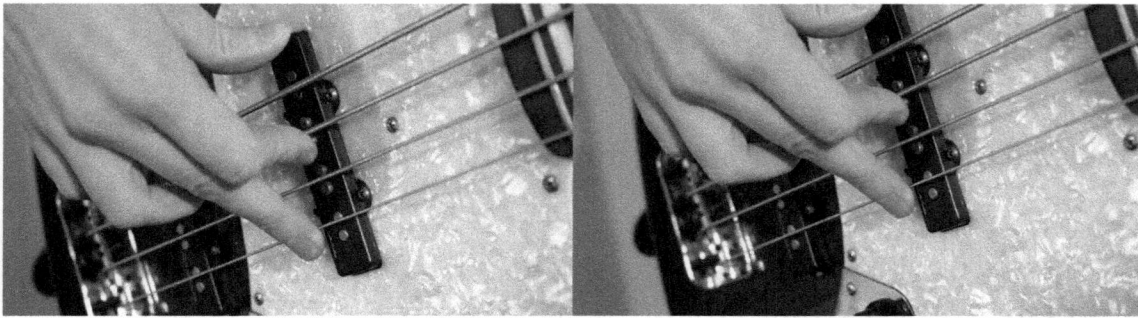

- o Do not play from above – this will create fret noises and reduce sustain.
- o Do not play from underneath the string either (an approach known as 'freestyle' in classical guitar technique) – this creates fret noise, doesn't mute the next string, and is not as efficient

3. **Keep your finger distance from the strings to a minimum (Approximately 1/4 inch away from the string being played). This is an unnecessary use of energy and will slow your playing down in the long run. Excessive force from momentum is not required to create a good tone, and avoiding large distances will help with fret buzz as well.**

4. **On the E string, your finger should gently roll across the top of E string and come to rests against the pad of your thumb that is resting on the pickup.**

Note:

More advanced players may wish to consider trying the "floating thumb" concept, which will be explained in a subsequent volume.

With this concept, the thumb "floats" to rest on whatever string is below the one you are currently playing on, rather than resting on the pickup or in some other stationary position.

This technique helps to mute the unused strings and means that you do not need to stretch your hand to play the higher strings. The floating thumb technique can improve your playing speed and reduce fatigue.

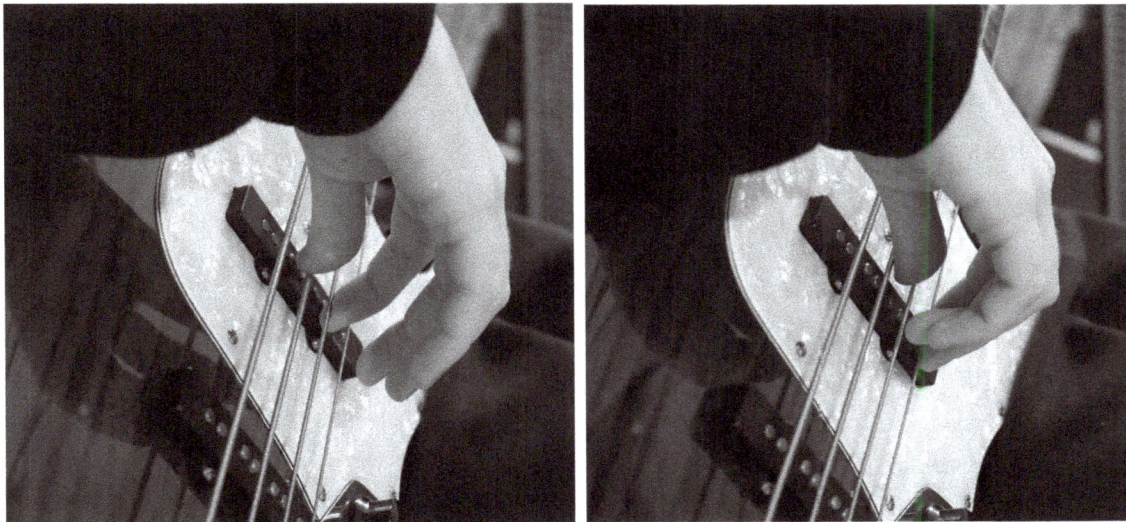

Caption: The "Floating Thumb" technique

1. Keep your fingernails short, at least on your playing fingers (index and middle). Long fingernails will produce an unpleasant ticking noise against the strings. Choose to use a pick instead of long fingernails if you want to achieve this tone.

2. Pinky and ring fingers move sympathetically to the index and middle fingers – they do not need to be held in any particular position – leave them be

3. Play lightly, too much force will give a distorted sound and will waste your energy. However, not enough pressure will produce a thin, inconsistent tone, so it is important to find the right balance.

4. The idea is to glide your finger across the string. Do not pull up on the strings.

Exercise to Try

To practice right hand finger technique, ignore your left hand and have your right hand play slow quarter notes on open strings. Use this checklist:

1. Rolling your fingers across the string and muting next strings
2. Using the ball of the finger to contact string
3. Applying enough pressure to get solid tone
4. Don't hit strings, roll across
5. Rolling finger on E string into thumb resting on pickup
6. Practice alternating between the two fingers and creating a consistent tone
7. Don't pull up on strings

Picking / Pick Style

For rock or metal, you may choose to use a pick instead of your fingers. The pick provides a clear, gritty, distinct sound.

There are three thicknesses for picks: thin (.40 and .60 mm), medium (.60 to .80 mm), and heavy (anything past .80 mm). Heavy is theoretically best for bass because it will not flex when a string is played. However, a heavy string may not be flexible enough, so see which pick works best for you.

The two most common materials used for picks are plastic or nylon. However, there are a lot of other materials to choose from, such as: tortoise shell, DuPont Delrin, Cellulose Acetate Nitrate, Ultem (polyetherimide), polymerized animal protein, stone, wood, leather, and other exotic materials.

The shape of picks can differ too, and as your playing develops, you may gravitate to a certain shape you find desirable. Types of shapes include: fin shaped, equilateral triangle, standard rounded point, teardrop, etc. A couple pick suggestions for bass include a Fender Heavy or a nylon Herco by Dunlop.

You can pick using a **Downstroke**, picking towards the floor, or an **Upstroke**, picking towards yourself/upwards.

1. Practice downstrokes initially on G string to get a feel for the pick

2. Hold pick between thumb and first finger, using pointed edge to pick string:

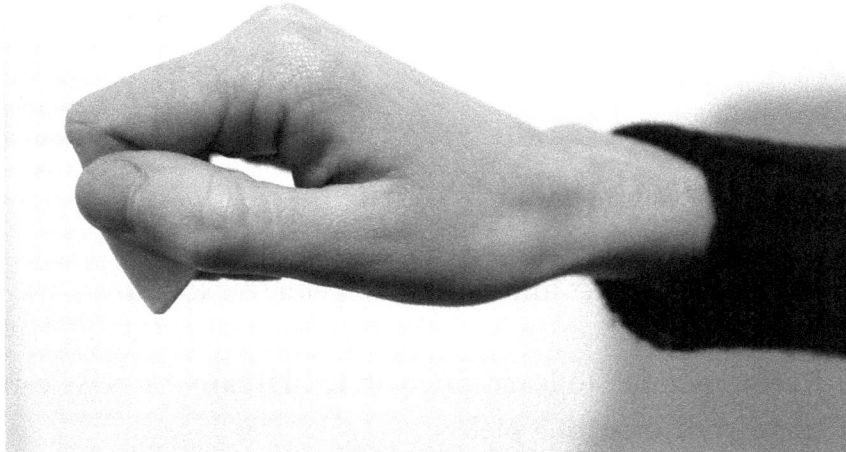

3. Make sure pick is flat against string, do not use edge of pick

4. Rest pinky on bass or on lower edge of pickup

5. Avoid extreme bending in wrist

6. Make sure pick connects fully to get a full sound

7. Recommended to learn fingerstyle first, any exercise can be played either fingerstyle or with a pick

The Left Hand!

Left Hand Finger Numbering

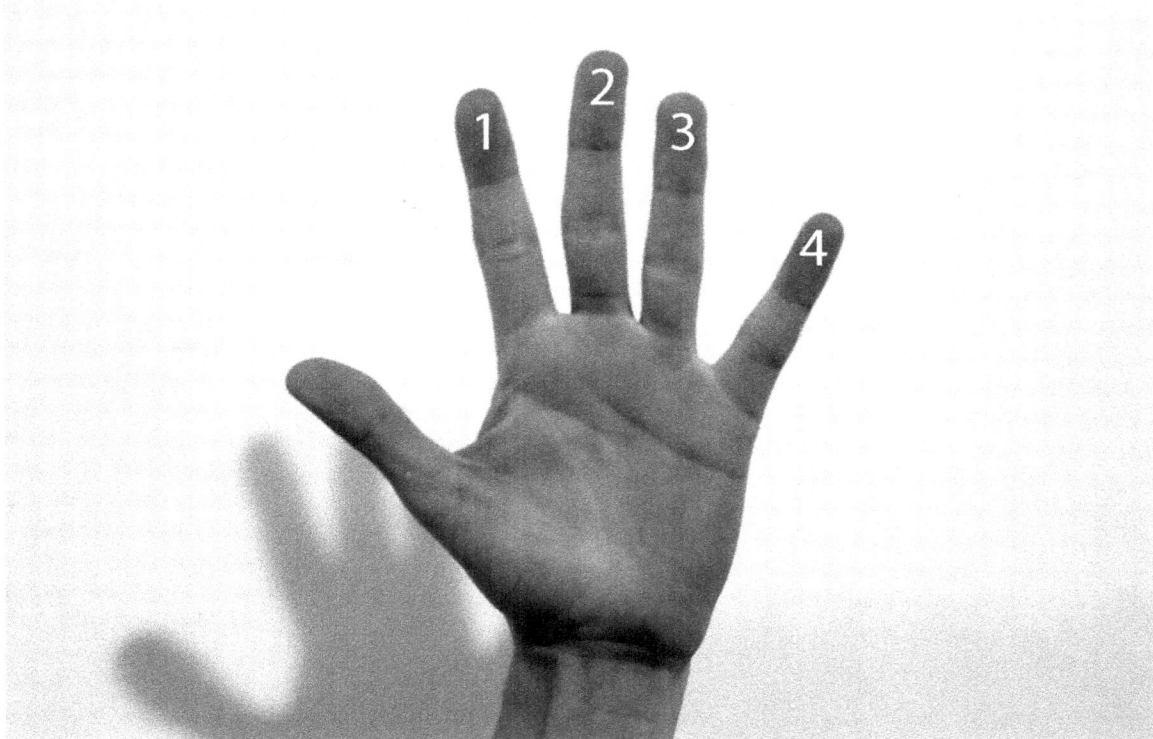

The pad of your thumb should be roughly in the middle/center of the back of the bass neck, roughly behind your index and middle fingers. Your thumb will helps your fingers to press down firmly on the strings to produce a quality tone and reduce any fret buzz.

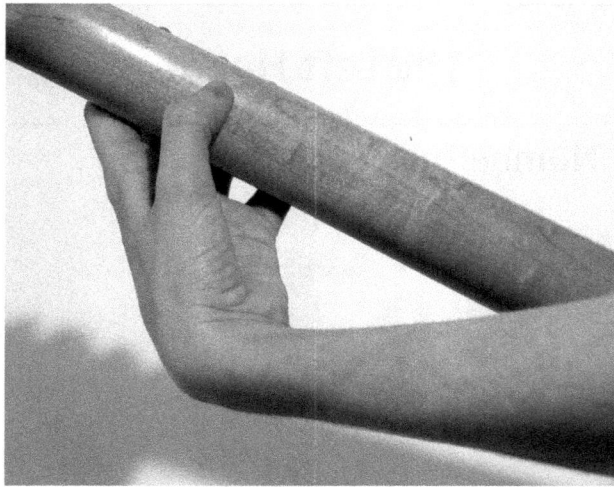

Make sure your thumb does not stick up or hook over the top of the bass, as this does not support the fretting action of your fingers:

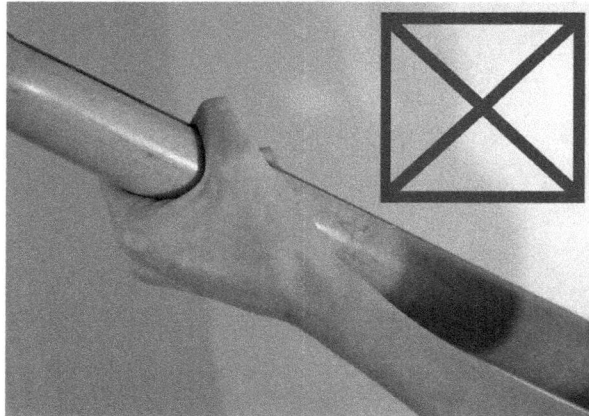

Use the flat area at ends of your fingers to press down on the strings – do not use your fingertips. Using the flat part of your fingers means that you can stretch your fingers wider across more of the fretboard. Additionally, using the flat part of your fingers can help to mute upper strings that may be left unprotected otherwise if you were using your fingertips.

Always press down to the far right of every fret, directly behind the fret – if you do not do this, the note will inevitably buzz. This also requires less energy to hold down the string and will give you better intonation.

Do not arch your fingers too much as this will likely cause you to play with your fingertips instead of the flat area of your fingers. Using your fingertips restricts your span of reach in the left hand.

Make sure your fingers do not collapse when pressing down on the frets:

Keep fingers close to string and avoid removing any fingers from their playing position:

Fingers should remain parallel to frets and in position as much as possible.

Spread your fingers out as much as you can, don't bunch them together!

First Position

First finger on first fret, second finger on second fret and third and fourth fingers on third fret

1. Both third and fourth finger play together. The third finger is used to support your fourth finger initially until you build up strength. Eventually, you will use one finger per fret.

Caption: First Position

2. Keep the note ringing until you are ready to start the next one. Don't stop the note – sustain it for as long as possible so that it smoothly connects to the next note. In musical notation, this is called *legato.*

3. Keep your left hand relaxed as much as possible – do not hold a position that feels strained, and try to avoid any extreme bending in your wrist.

CHAPTER

Tablature and Musical Notation

I n this chapter we will touch on a basic overview of the two different systems of notation for electric bass: tablature and musical notation. We will explain what tablature is and how to read it, and we will go over some of the very basics of music theory to get us started.

Tablature

Tablature, or TAB, is a system of music notation that is unique to bass and guitar. You don't have to learn how to read the musical staff with tab as it tells you exactly where to find each note on the fretboard.

In this book, the TAB will be given under the traditional musical notation. Use the TAB notation to help you learn how to read the staff. Tablature will be phased out in subsequent volumes.

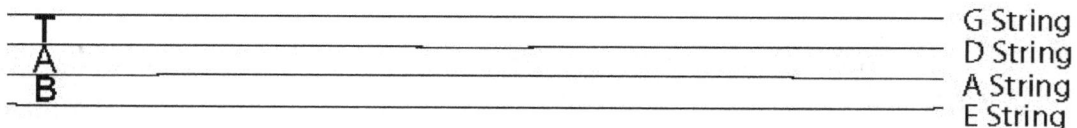

```
T ─────────────────────────────────────────── G String
A ─────────────────────────────────────────── D String
B ─────────────────────────────────────────── A String
  ─────────────────────────────────────────── E String
```

Lines represent open (not fretted) strings on the bass. The lowest line represents the bottom E string, and the highest line is the top G string.

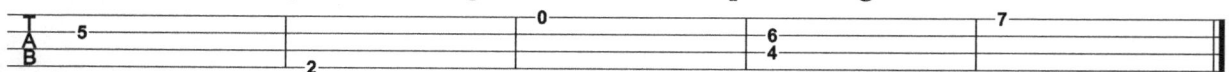

```
T ───────────────0───────────────────7─────
A 5───────────────────────6──────────────────
B ───────2──────────────────4────────────────
```

The numbers on the lines indicate which fret to press down on that string.
Tab often does not give rhythm, so you may need to refer to the staff for that.

Musical Staff (Stave):

Although TAB is easy to read, it is not the traditional way to write music. The musical staff is 5 lines, and notes are written on the lines and the spaces in between these lines.

This is called the Grand Staff. It is a combination of both the treble and bass clefs.

Clefs:

Music for bass is written in Bass Clef, sometimes referred to as the F Clef:

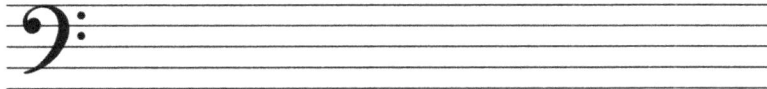

Anther common clef, the Treble Clef, is used for guitar as well as many other instruments:

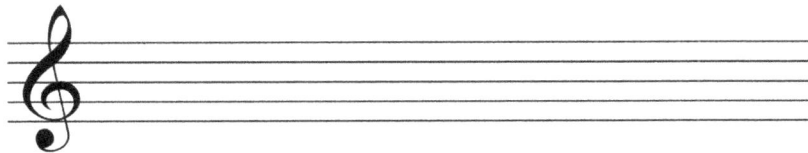

The Musical alphabet is A B C D E F G. After G, this sequence repeats.

The notes on the lines of the Bass clef are G B D F & A in ascending order. A good way to remember them is with the acronym, Good Boys Deserve Fudge Always!

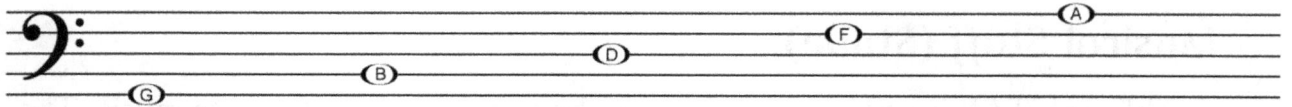

The notes in the spaces of the Bass clef are A C E & G. You can use the acronym, All Cows Eat Grass to help remember them!

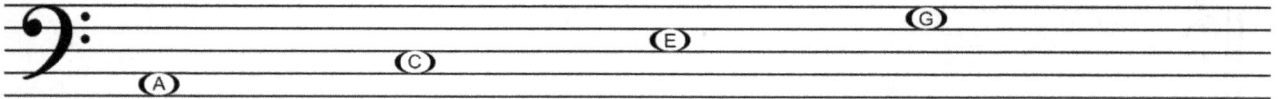

Measures, sometimes referred to as bars, contain a specific number of beats. Bar lines separate measures.

Double bar lines show the end of a section of a piece of music.

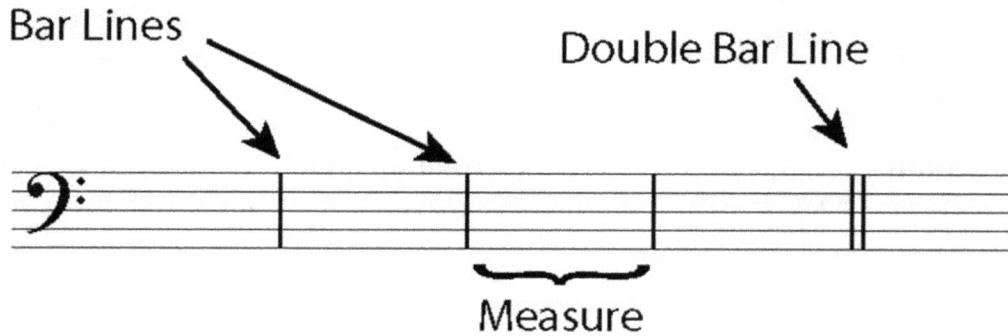

A final bar line shows the end of a piece of music:

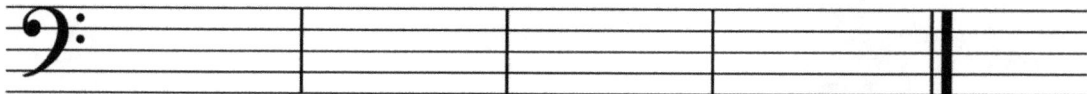

Time Signatures

Time signatures indicate the number of beats in each measure and appear at the start of the music, after the clef:

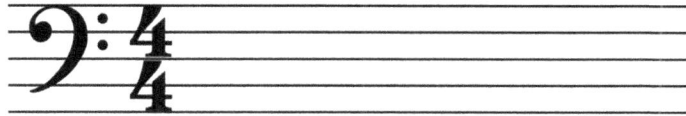

The top number signifies how many beats are in a bar. The bottom number signifies which type of note receives one beat (i.e. in $\frac{4}{4}$ – a quarter note gets 1 beat).

In this book we will be using $\frac{3}{4}$ and $\frac{4}{4}$. In $\frac{3}{4}$ time there is 3 beats in each measure and a quarter note receives one beat.

Note Values

Quarter Note = 1 beat

Quarter Note Count

1   2   3   4

Half Note = 2 beats

Half Note Count

1   2   3   4

Dotted Half Note = 3 beats

Note: A dot after a note or a rest increases its value by one-half.

Dotted Half-Note Count

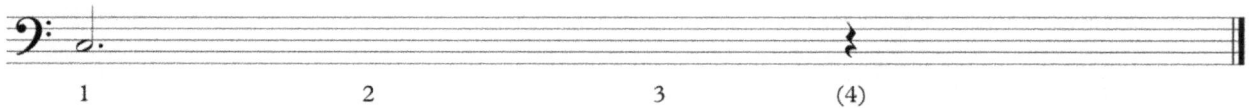

1   2   3   (4)

Whole Note = 4 beats

Whole Note Count

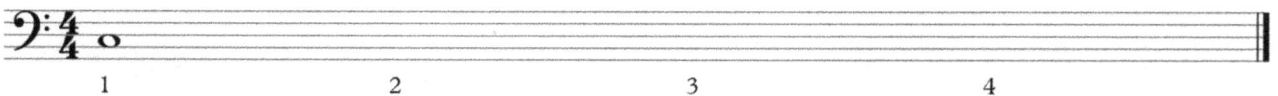

1   2   3   4

When Reading music or tab, get into the habit of tapping your foot along to the beat!

Rests

A rest is a measured silence in a piece of music.

Quarter Note Rest = 1 beat of silence

Half Note Rest = 2 beats of silence

Whole Note Rest = 4 beats of silence

To achieve a rest with your bass, you can stop the string vibrations by placing the fingers of your left hand over the string without pressing them down. Or, you can stop the sound using the fingers of your right hand in a similar fashion.

CHAPTER

4

Let's Play!

In chapter 4 we will go through some simple exercises on each string individually on the bass guitar. We will also continue to gain knowledge about music theory as we go along, and will learn some techniques to help with our playing. We will have the opportunity to start playing some tunes once we start to become familiar with our instrument.

Counting on Open Strings

Quarter Notes

Half Notes

Whole Notes

Raking

When moving down to lower strings (i.e. towards yourself, not away) use the same right hand finger to play both strings consecutively as you move down.

Raking Example

i = index finger
m = middle finger

This is a technique called raking that is used on descending adjacent strings (i.e. G to D or A to E). Both fingers can be equally involved. Raking makes playing easier as it helps your right hand relaxed as you move down to the lower string, and means that you do not have to alternate fingers as much. Raking is more fluid than always alternating fingers.

As you get more advanced, more than two strings can be raked.

Notes on the G String

Sharps and Flats

When a sharp sign (♯) is put in front of a note, it means that you need to raise the pitch of the note up a half-step (semitone) by playing that note one fret higher than usual. For example, if the note is usually played on the 1ˢᵗ fret, play the sharp note on the 2ⁿᵈ fret. Or if the note is usually played on an open string, play the sharp note on the 1ˢᵗ fret.

When a flat sign (♭) is put in front of a note, it means you need to lower the pitch of that note down a half-step (semitone) by playing that note one fret lower than usual. For example, if the note usually played on the 2ⁿᵈ fret, play the flat note on the first fret. If the note is usually played on the 3ʳᵈ fret, play the flat on the 2ⁿᵈ fret, and so on.

To flat a note that is usually played on an open string, play the 4ᵗʰ fret of the next lower string.

When a natural sign (♮) is placed in front of a note, it cancels any previous sharps or flats that had previously been put on the note. It means the note can be played 'naturally,' as is, without making it sharp or flat. Sometimes natural signs are placed in the following measure as a reminder.

A note only needs to be indicated sharp or flat at the beginning of each bar, so you have to remember which notes are sharps and flats throughout the remainder of a bar.

In musical notation, sharps are usually used when ascending in pitch, and flats are used when descending.

G Am G Bm Am Bm G
G Bm Am Bm Am G Am G
Am B♭m Bm Am G
Bm Am G
G♯m7(♭5) G♯m7(♭5) C7(♯5) C7(♯5) Fm6/9
G Am G Am A♭7 G

Notes on D String

Notes on the D and G Strings:

Dinor Blues

Major Plans

Minor D-Tales

The Tie

The tie is a curved line between two notes with the same pitch. The duration of both notes get "tied" together so that one longer note is played instead. The second note in a tie is not played but held.

Example with Tie:

3D

Up and Down Stems

The stems of notes can be either pointing up or down, depending on where they are placed on the staff. Notes that are above or on the middle line have their stems facing down.

Notes that are below the middle line have their stems facing up.

Having the stems pointing up and down this way makes the music look tidier and thus easier to read!

Notes on A String

A Team

A and D String Exercises

Minor Walk

Penta-Chromatic

Royal D Duet

This next tune can be played as a duet with your teacher. You can play the first part and your teacher can play along with you using the second part!

Student Part:

Teacher Part:

Notes on E string

E string is largest and most difficult string to play because you have to press down harder than the other strings. Make sure you press close to the fret (without being on it).

Ledger Lines

A ledger line is a short line that extends the staff down or upward. Ledger lines are used to indicate pitches that are below or above the regular lines or spaces of the musical staff. The bottom open E string of the bass is notated on a ledger line.

If note is too high/low, use ledger line:

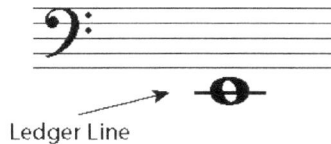

Ledger Line

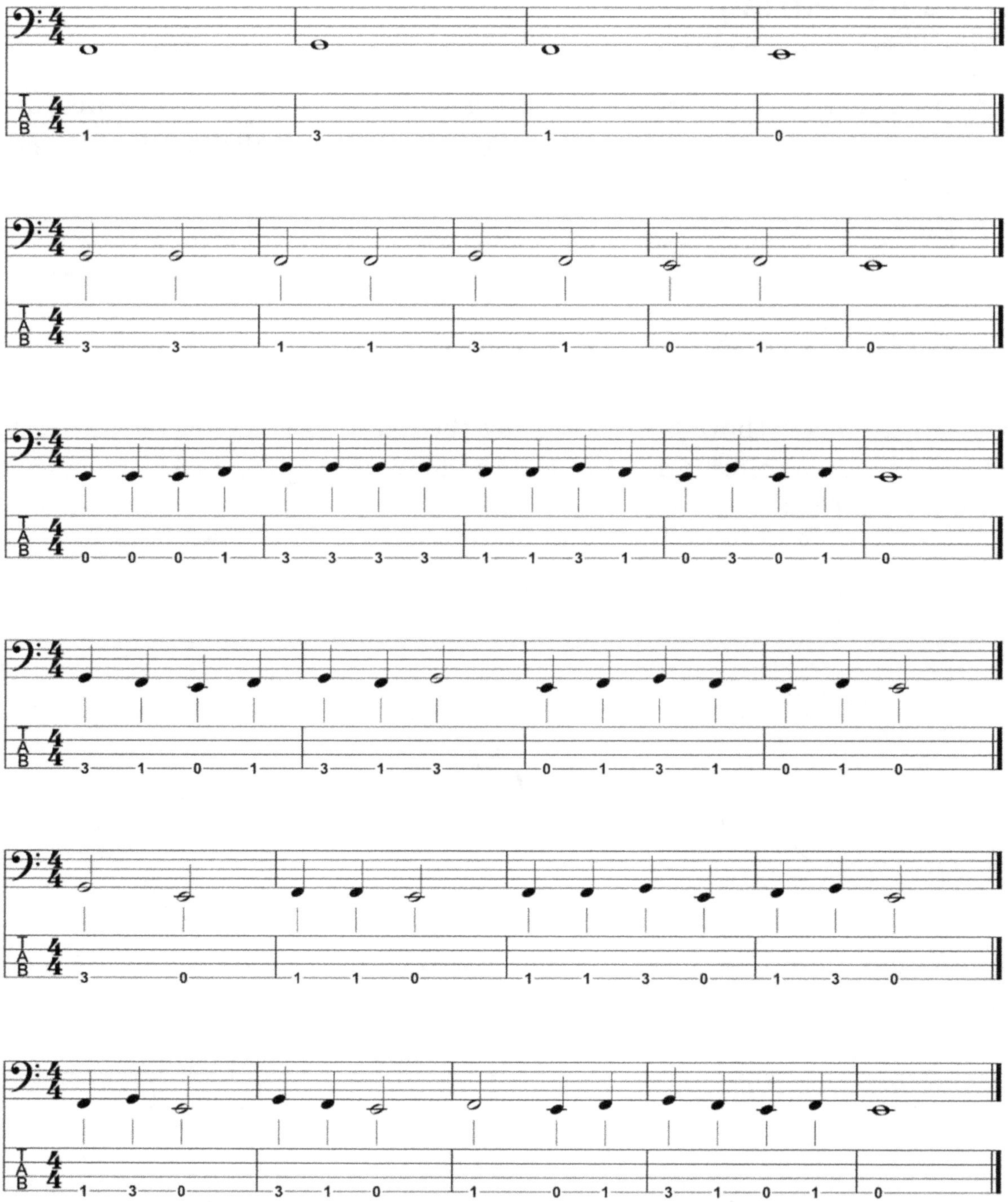

Shifting from 1st to 2nd Position

In order to play all the notes in the following exercise, you must shift from 1st to 2nd position. You can shift using any finger. Try some of the examples below.

E-Z Street

E-Z Street II

E and A String Exercises

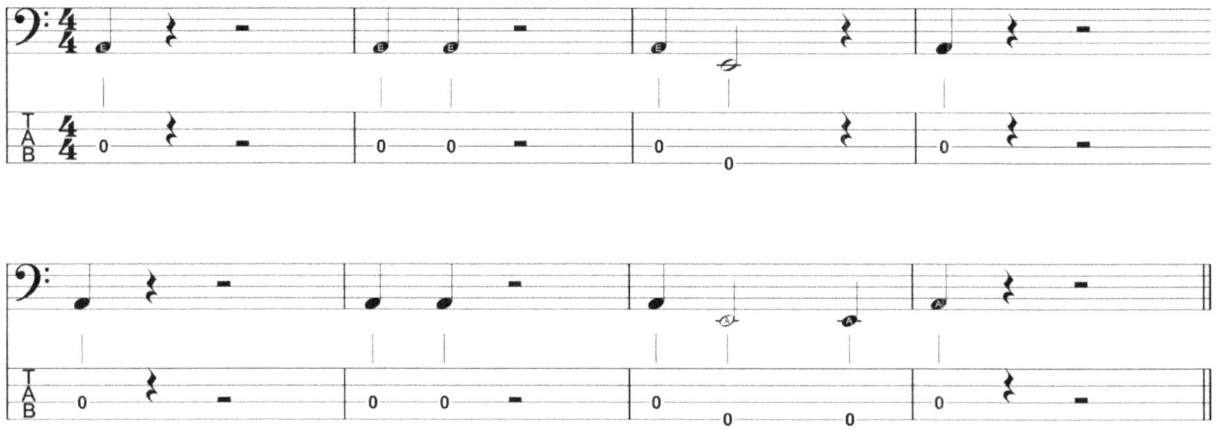

Three's Company

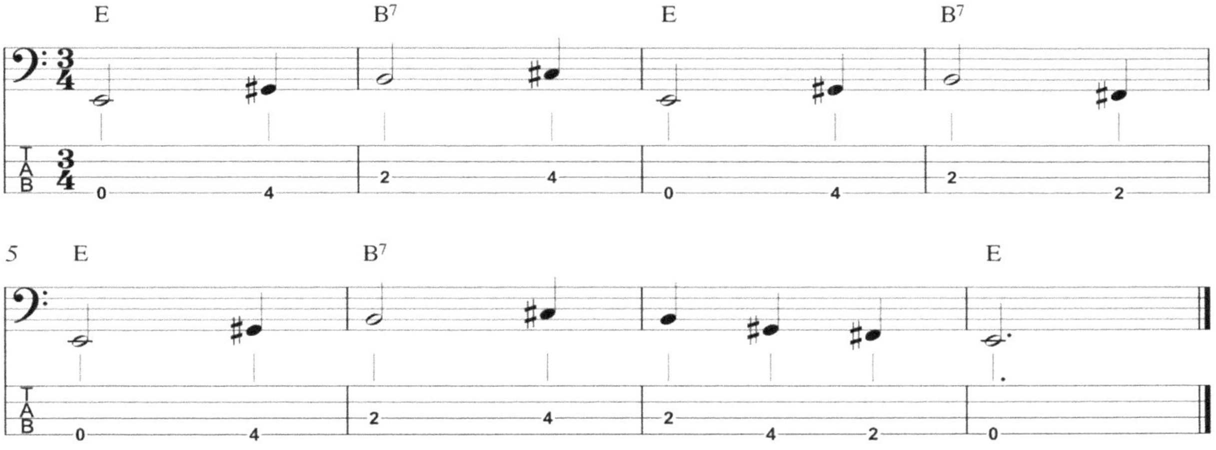

Acer

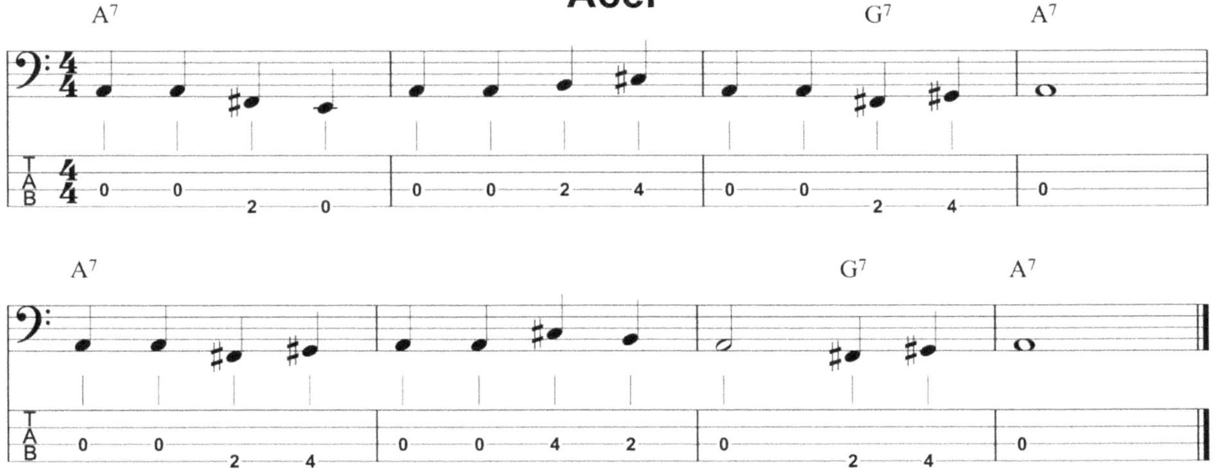

A and D Strings

Repeat Sign

The repeat sign is used to indicate that a section of music must be repeated. When you reach the repeat sign, go back to the beginning and play it again!

1st and 2nd Endings

1st and 2nd endings are indicated with brackets and the numbers "1" and "2." When you reach this part of the music, you must play through the 1st ending, treating it like a repeat sign, and going back to the beginning. Play through until you reach the same section but this time choose the 2nd ending and skip the 1st ending! Sometimes there can be even more than 2 endings!

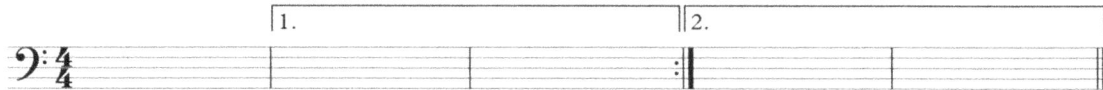

CHAPTER

5

All Strings, Octaves and Eighth Notes

Now that we have learned how to play each string individually, lets try putting them all together. We will also explore the concept of the "octave" and learn about another rhythmic permutation called the "eighth note."

At the end of this chapter, students have the option to play through the final reading test as a way to gauge their learning thus far.

E, A and D Strings

Collective Blues

Chain of Cool

Narrow Bolero

The Octave

An octave is the same note up or down 8 letters in the musical alphabet. The musical alphabet as we know goes A B C D E F G and then repeats up or down in either direction. Therefore, The next A up or down from the first A in the alphabet is it's octave: A - B - C - D - E - F - G - A ← this A is the octave of the first A. The octave is a very common musical pattern in bass playing.

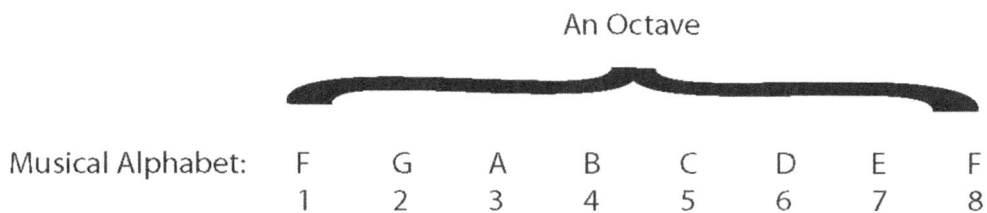

The pattern for playing an octave on the bass is consistent throughout the fretboard. It is always 2 frets over and 2 strings up or down from any note on the E or A string.

Example:

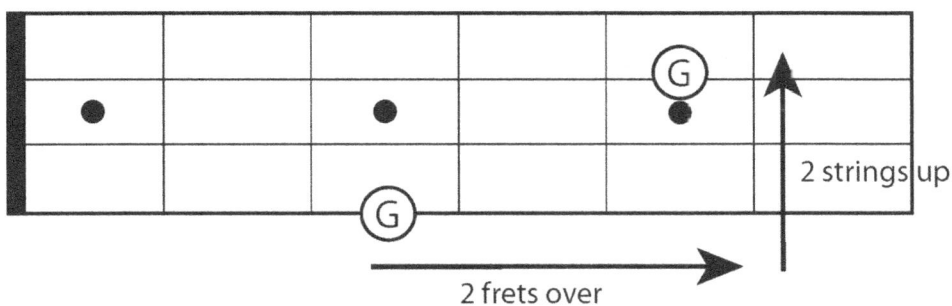

Octa-Gone

Queen Bee

Rock Around the Clock

All Strings Attached

Eighth Notes

Up until now we have been focusing on whole notes, half notes, quarter notes and dotted quarter notes. But there are other types of notes! We will now introduce the *Eighth Note*, a note that receives half a beat or count. When you divide a quarter note in half, you get two eighth notes.

Eighth notes are black notes with a flag added to the stem, to differentiate them from quarter notes. Groups of two or more eighth notes are joined together using beams.

Caption: An Eighth Note

Caption: Two or more Eighth Notes are joined together with a beam

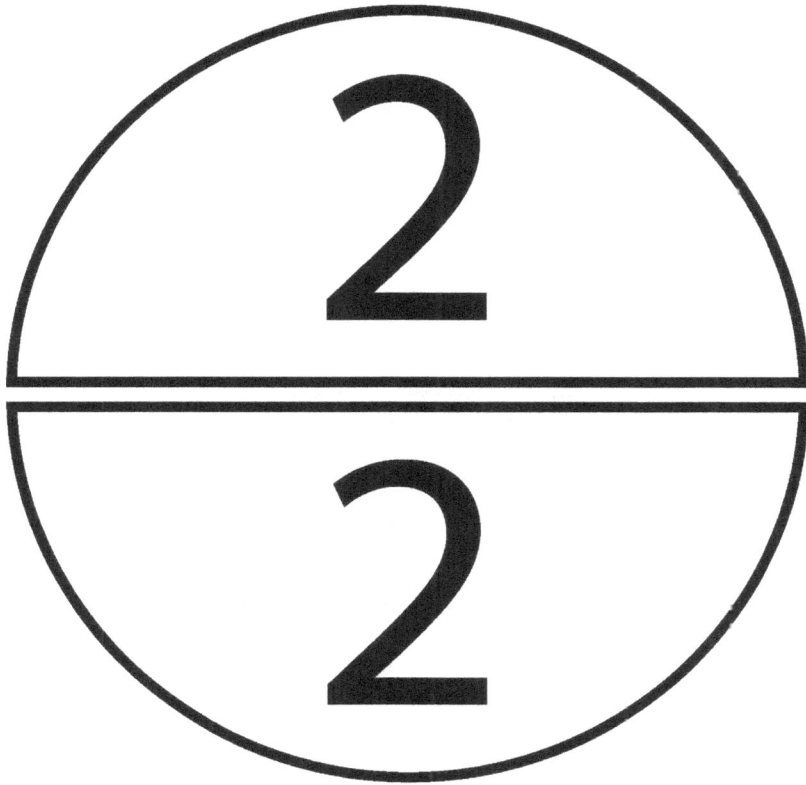

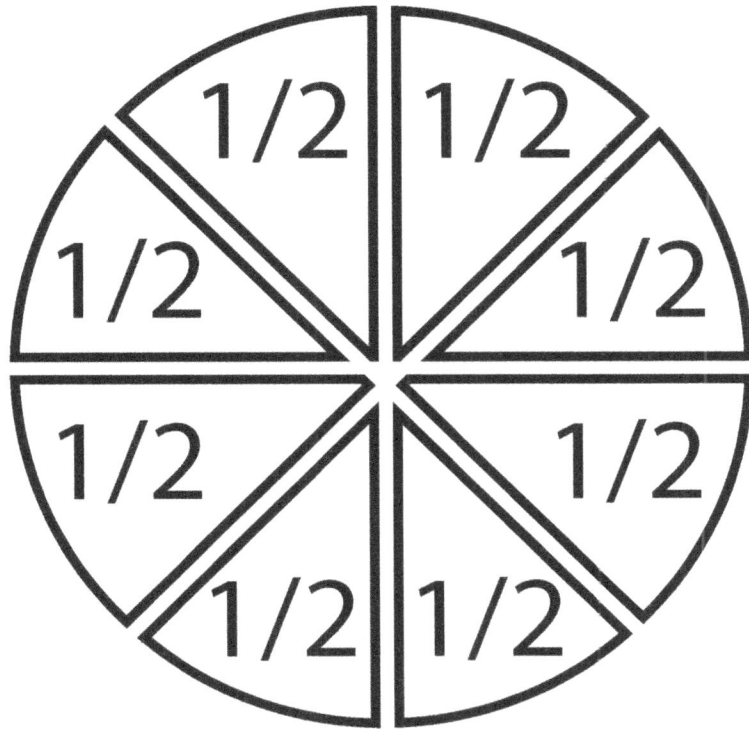

Line Drive

Minor Blues

Sunshine

Final Reading Test

Bonus Section

6

Rhythmic Exercises

Each volume will have a selection of rhythmic exercises to practice reading. Put your bass down for the following exercises where we will spend some time reading rhythms.

Always use a metronome for these exercises and ideally, for all practicing. Strive for accuracy, not speed.

Practice counting these rhythms out loud and tapping your foot with the pulse.

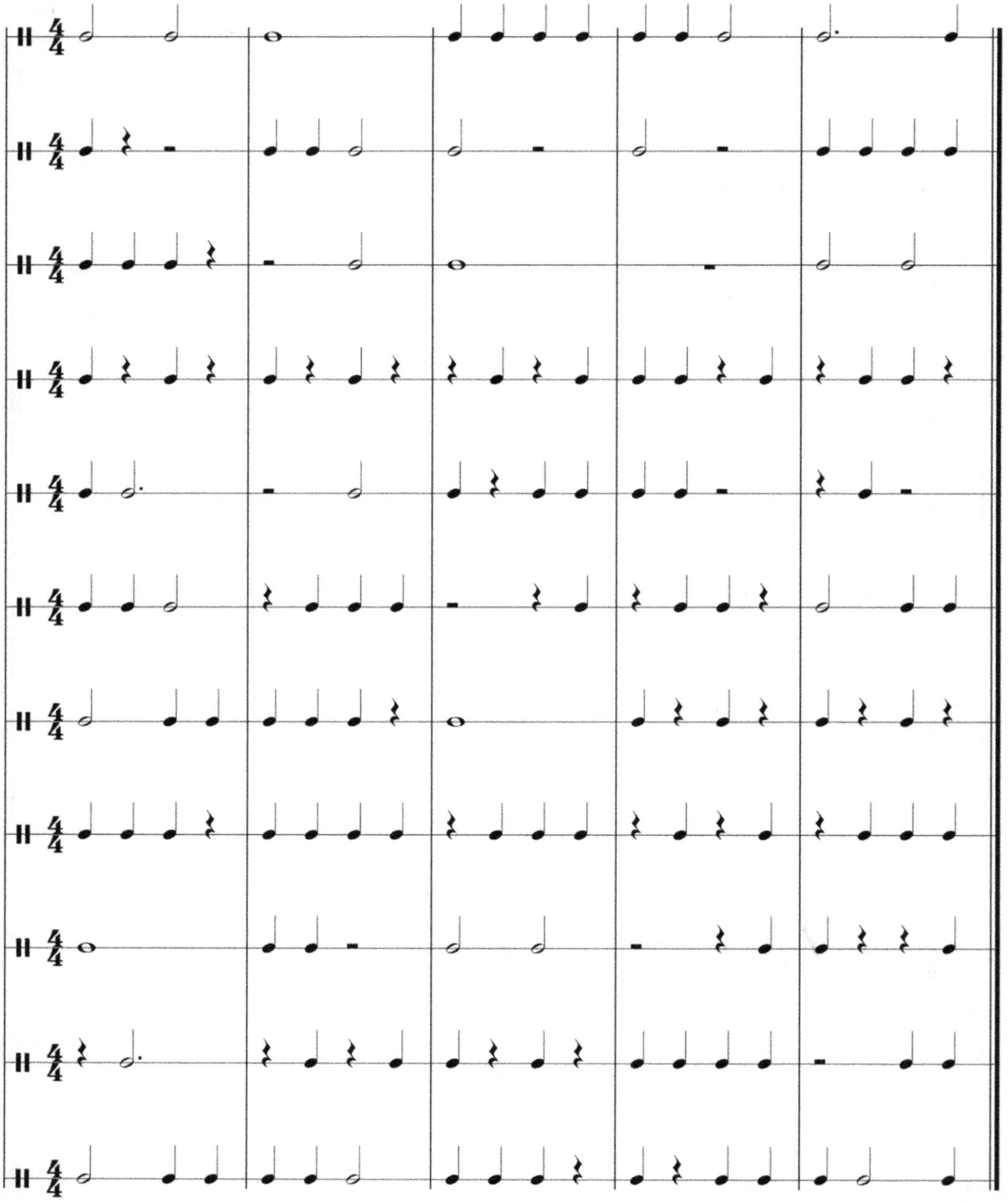

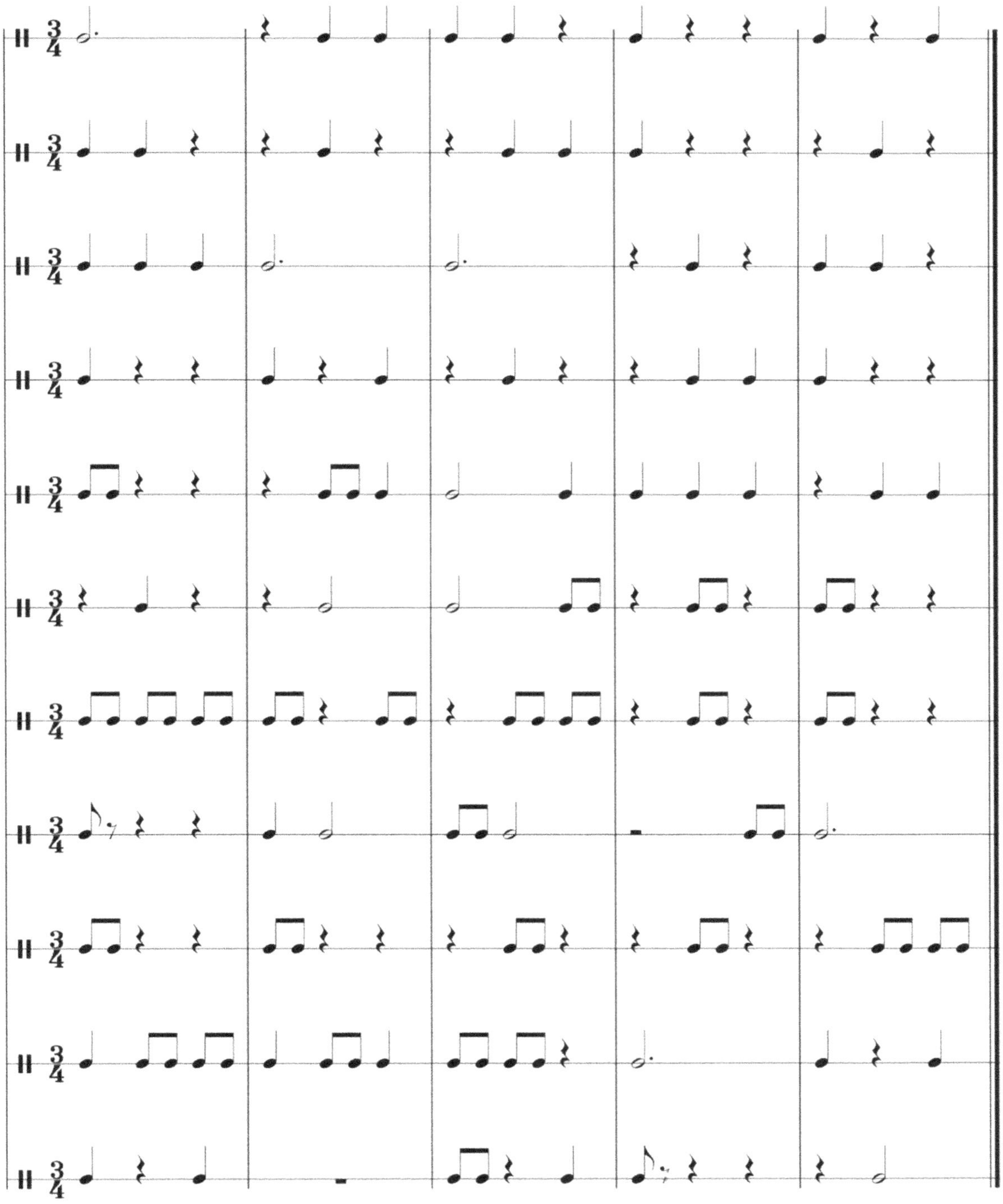

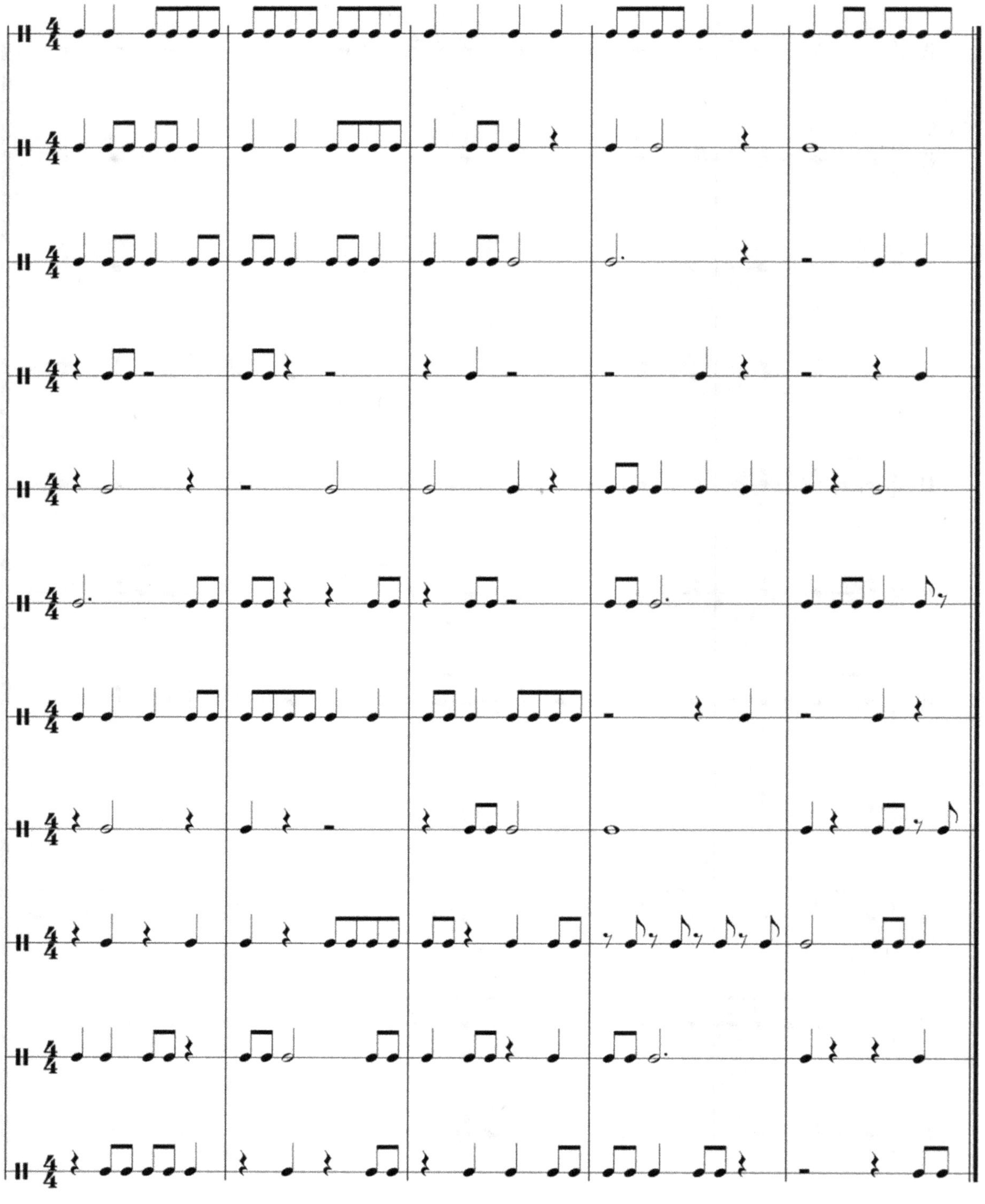

CHAPTER

Ear Training Exercises

In this final chapter, we will practice training our ears. We will be learning to indicate and differentiate the types of rhythms we hear, and we will also   practice hearing the differences between $\frac{3}{4}$ and $\frac{4}{4}$ time signatures. The answers to each exercise will appear at the back of the book.

1. Your teacher will clap a rhythmic pattern. Circle the pattern that you hear.

e. Or

f. Or

g. Or

2. Your teacher will clap two rhythm patterns. Circle whether you think the patterns are the same or different.

a. Same   Different   b. Same   Different

c. Same   Different   d. Same   Different

e. Same   Different   f. Same   Different

g. Same   Different   h. Same   Different

3. Your teacher will play melodies in $\frac{3}{4}$ or $\frac{4}{4}$ time. Circle whether you think the melody is being played in $\frac{3}{4}$ or $\frac{4}{4}$.

a. $\frac{3}{4}$ $\frac{4}{4}$

b. $\frac{3}{4}$ $\frac{4}{4}$

c. $\frac{3}{4}$ $\frac{4}{4}$

d. $\frac{3}{4}$ $\frac{4}{4}$

e. $\frac{3}{4}$ $\frac{4}{4}$

f. $\frac{3}{4}$ $\frac{4}{4}$

g. $\frac{3}{4}$ $\frac{4}{4}$

h. $\frac{3}{4}$ $\frac{4}{4}$

Teacher's Examples:

1. Clap these examples

2. Clap these examples

a.

b.

c.

d.

e.

f.

g.

h.

3. Play these melodies

a.

b.

c.

d.

e.

f.

g.

h.

ABOUT THE AUTHOR

Kaitie Sly is an award-winning bassist, singer-songwriter, music producer, and music educator. Originally from Canada, she started her career at the age of 8, performing in bars and clubs on Vancouver Island. She spent her formative years studying and performing on piano, bass and vocals. Sly began her studies at the Lebeau-Petersen Music Academy in Victoria, BC, where she eventually took over the role as bass instructor. In the early 2000's, Sly made television appearances on Much Music, with her band, Black Tie Social, as well as taught music, and performed at festivals, clubs and events with a plethora of other bands and artists. Growing up in Canada, Sly was fortunate enough to be able to share the stage with renowned artists such as Motown superstar, Martha Reeves, and has had many great performance highlights such as playing the famous Cavern Club in Liverpool, UK.

In 2009, Kaitie moved to the United States to attend the renowned Musicians Institute in Hollywood where she studied under some of LA's top session musicians. Here, she attained an Associates Degree in Bass Performance as well as the Outstanding Student Award upon graduating from her program. During her time at the Musicians Institute, she played bass for award-winning artists such as Mimi Page; Laura Vall of the Controversy, proclaimed one of the Hot 100 Best Independent Bands of 2012; and collaborated with television composer, Tomas Altamirano.

Since graduating from the Musicians Institute, Kaitie continues to work as a session bassist, music educator, and singer-songwriter in both Canada and the US and has been a featured artist on the player spotlight of notreble.com. As well, Sly writes original music and jingles that have been featured in videos and short films. Sly is currently recording her debut solo EP.

www.ingramcontent.com/pod-product-compliance
Lightning Source LLC
Chambersburg PA
CBHW081340090426
42737CB00017B/3220